Sirah Story M...

The Prophet Muhammad ﷺ
Migrates to Madinah

By
Saniyasnain Khan

Illustrated by Gurmeet

Goodwordkidz

Goodword Books Pvt. Ltd.
1, Nizamuddin West Market, New Delhi 110 013
e-mail: info@goodwordbooks.com   www.goodwordbooks.com

First published 2003   © Goodword Books 2004   Reprinted 2004   Printed in India

Five years after the beginning of the revelation of the Quran, a group of the Prophet's companions, weary of being tortured by the Makkans, left on the Prophet's advice to seek shelter in Abyssinia.

Find Makkah and Abyssinia on this map.
Also go from Start to Finish by visiting every place on this map.

© Goodword Books

Sirah Story Mazes: The Prophet Muhammad ﷺ Migrates to Madinah

When the Makkans learnt about the escape, they were very angry. They sent two very clever men to persuade King Negus, the Christian ruler of Abyssinia, to send the Muslims back. They carried many gifts with them.

On hearing the two clever Makkans' request, the king ordered the Muslims to appear before him. When the Muslims entered, they angered the king's advisors because they _____ to the king.

Trace the maze and fill in the blank to find out what made the king's advisors angry.

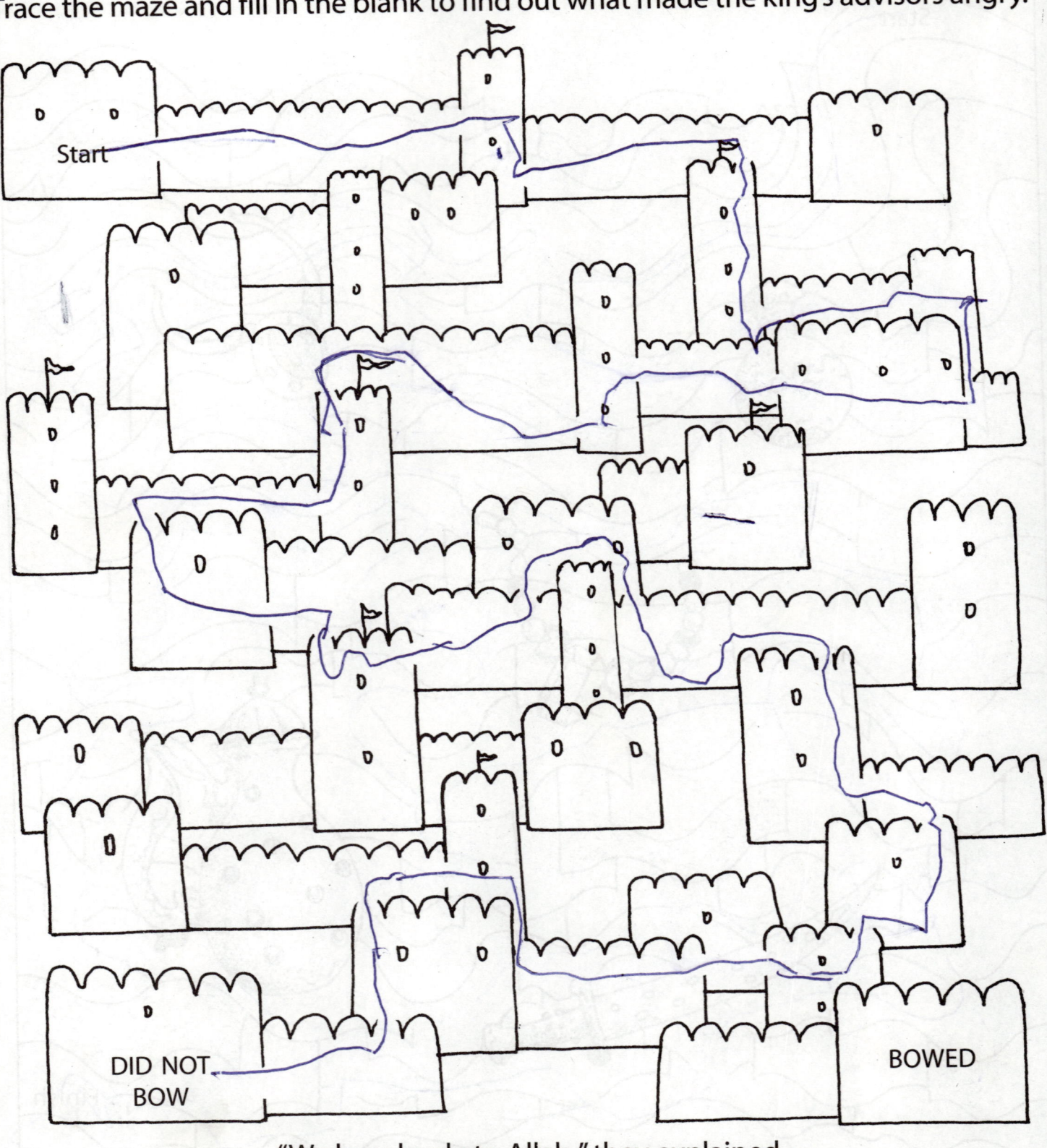

Start

DID NOT BOW

BOWED

"We kneel only to Allah," they explained.

© Goodword Books   4   Sirah Story Mazes: The Prophet Muhammad Migrates to Madinah

On hearing this, the excited King drew a line on the floor and exclaimed, "Between your religion and mine there is really no more difference than this line." With that he gave the Muslims permission to live peacefully in his realm.

Here are two mazes on the either side of a line.

© Goodword Books

7 Sirah Story Mazes: The Prophet Muhammad ﷺ Migrates to Madinah

In the meantime how were the Makkans treating the Prophet and his followers? Trace the maze and find out.

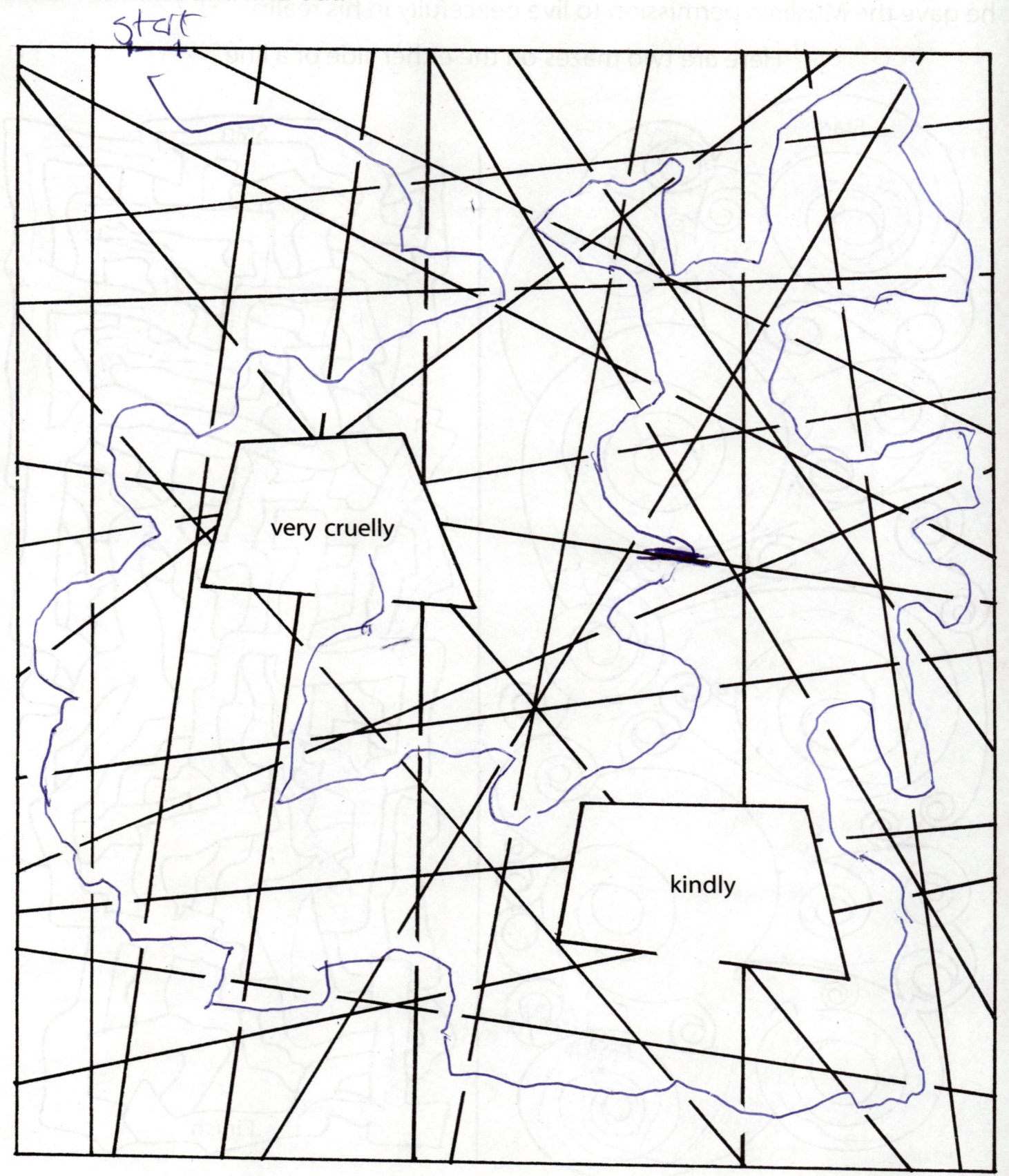

very cruelly

kindly

At this bitter moment, when the Quraysh, the rulers of Makkah, seemed to be about to crush Islam, the Prophet Muhammad ﷺ had an extraordinary experience. He was lifted up to the Heavens and brought into the presence of Allah. Which of these paths will lead to the heavens?

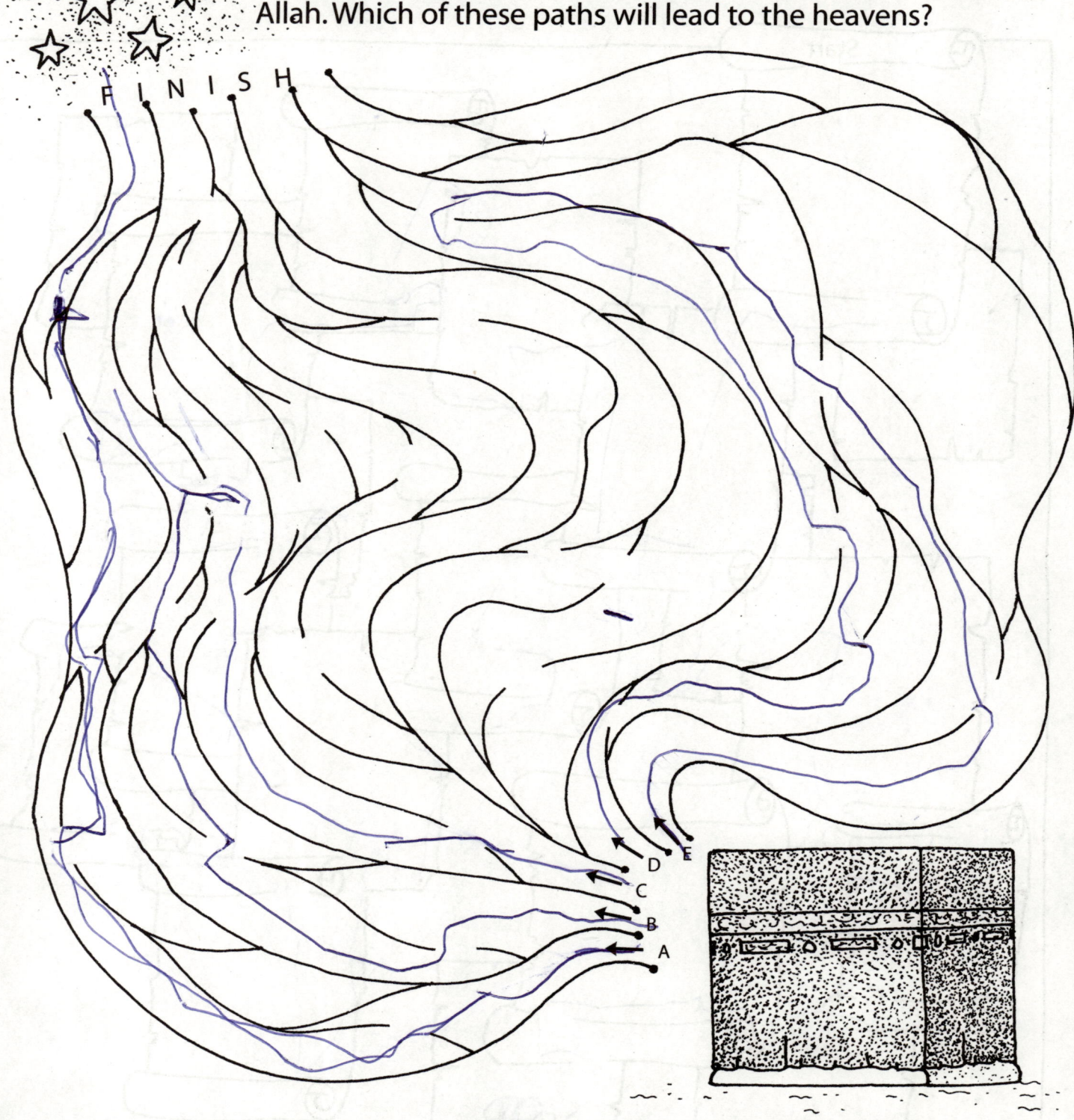

FINISH

A
B
C
D
E

This experience is called al-Isra and al-Mi'raj. This gave the Prophet ﷺ great comfort and strength to go on.

© Goodword Books

Sirah Story Mazes: The Prophet Muhammad ﷺ Migrates to Madinah

This and all the other important events in the Prophet's life, along with his observations and words of wisdom, were recorded by his Companions with great precision and faithfulness. These records came to be known as Hadith (traditions or sayings of the Prophet).

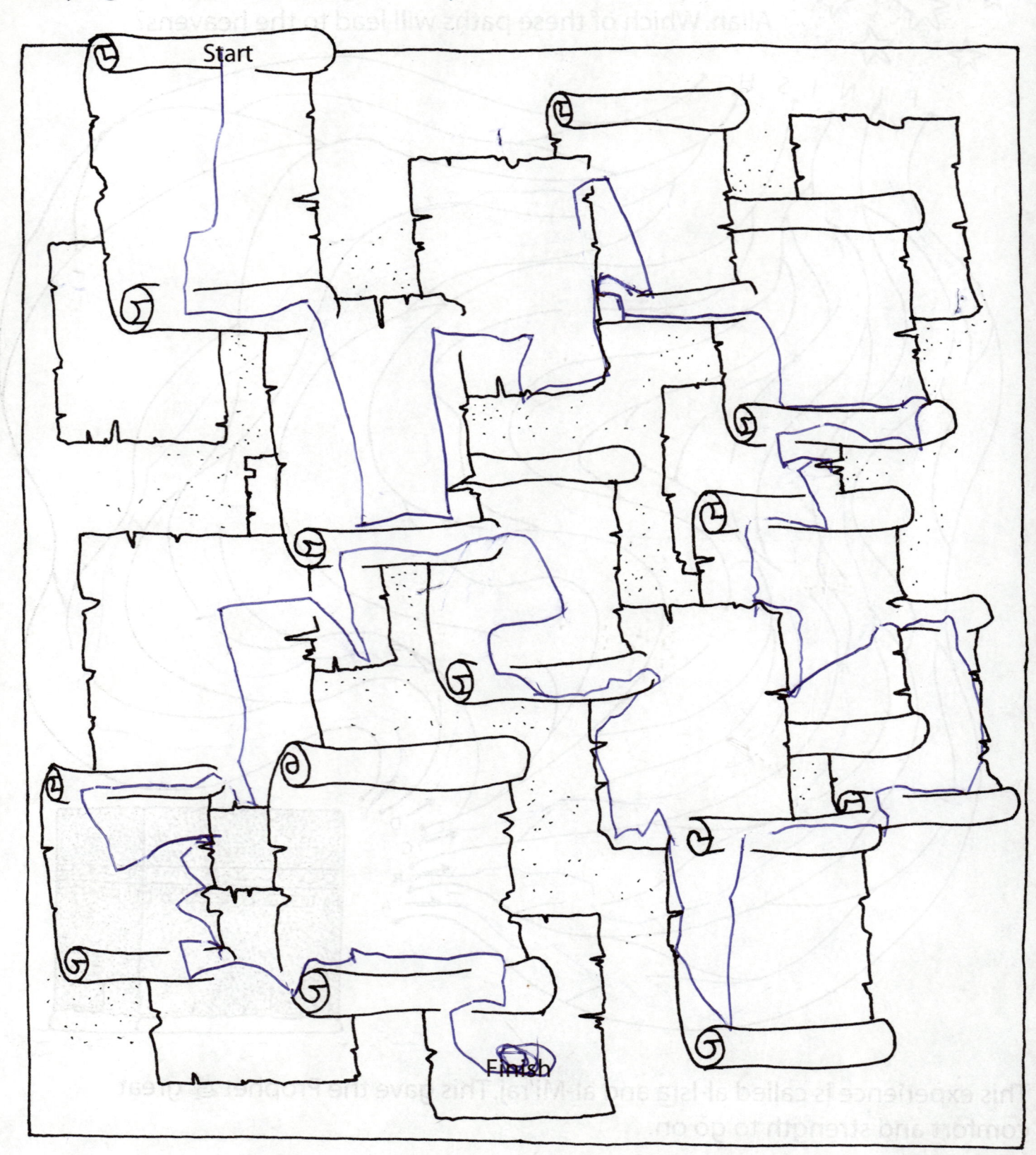

The Prophet's message was spreading far and wide. The Quraysh hatched a murder plot against him. Allah commanded him to leave Makkah and go to Madinah where he would be offered protection. Under the cover of darkness the Prophet and Abu Bakr slipped away on camel-back.

Start

Finish

© Goodword Books

11 Sirah Story Mazes: The Prophet Muhammad ﷺ Migrates to Madinah

When the Quraysh came to know, they sent out search parties to find them out. Guessing that the Prophet had gone towards Madinah in north, they went north. But the Prophet and Abu Bakr headed south.

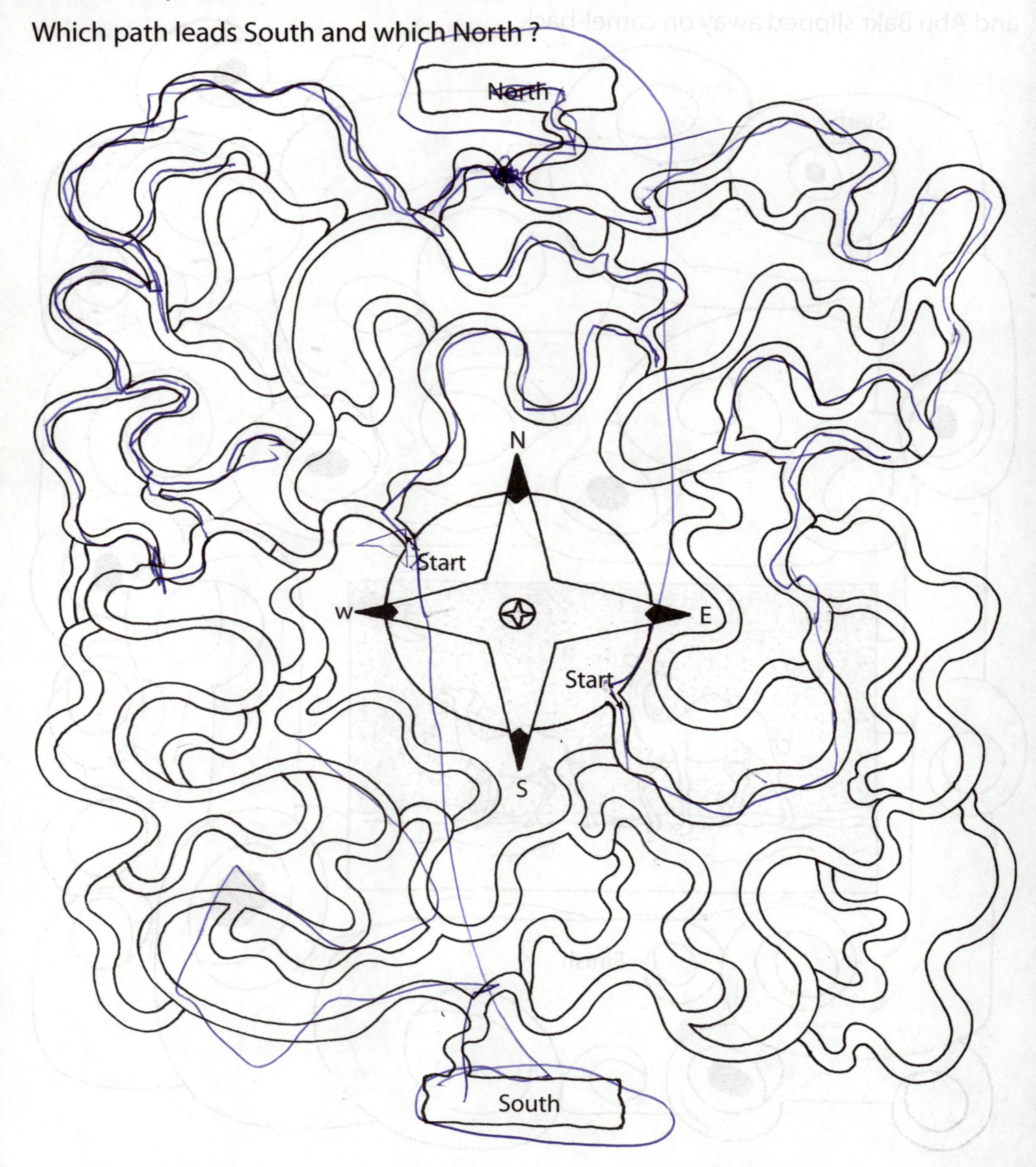

Which path leads South and which North?

They arranged that a shepherd would cover their tracks with his flock of sheep.
Can you reach Finish making your way about these sheep tracks?

They decided to hide in the Cave of Thawr, just outside Makkah.
Here solve these ten simple mazes quickly.
Find out which of these will lead to the cave.

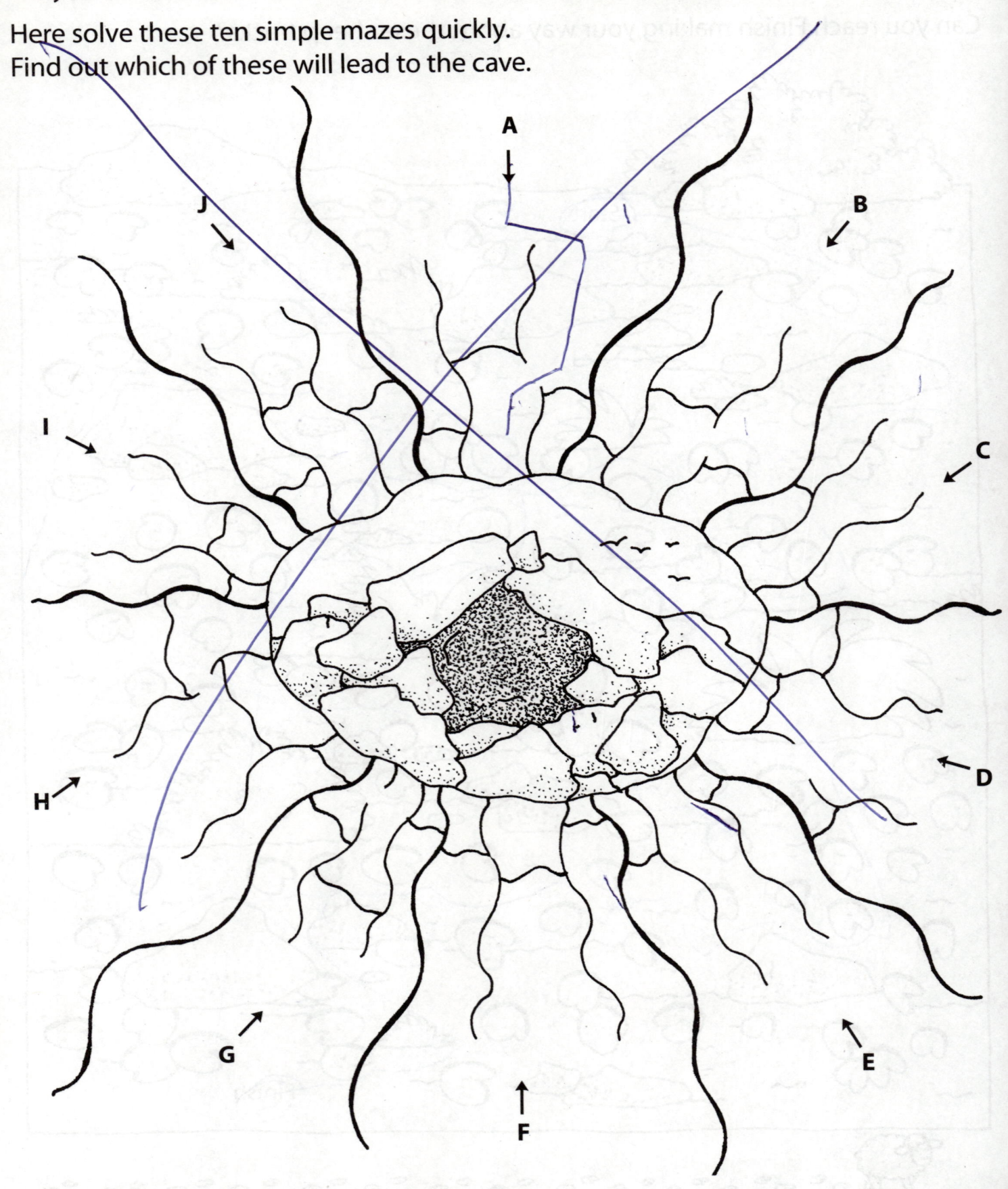

On the third day of hiding, they heard people approaching. Abu Bakr feared that they were going to be discovered. But the Prophet replied, "We are not two but three." Who was the third present with them? Trace the maze to find out.

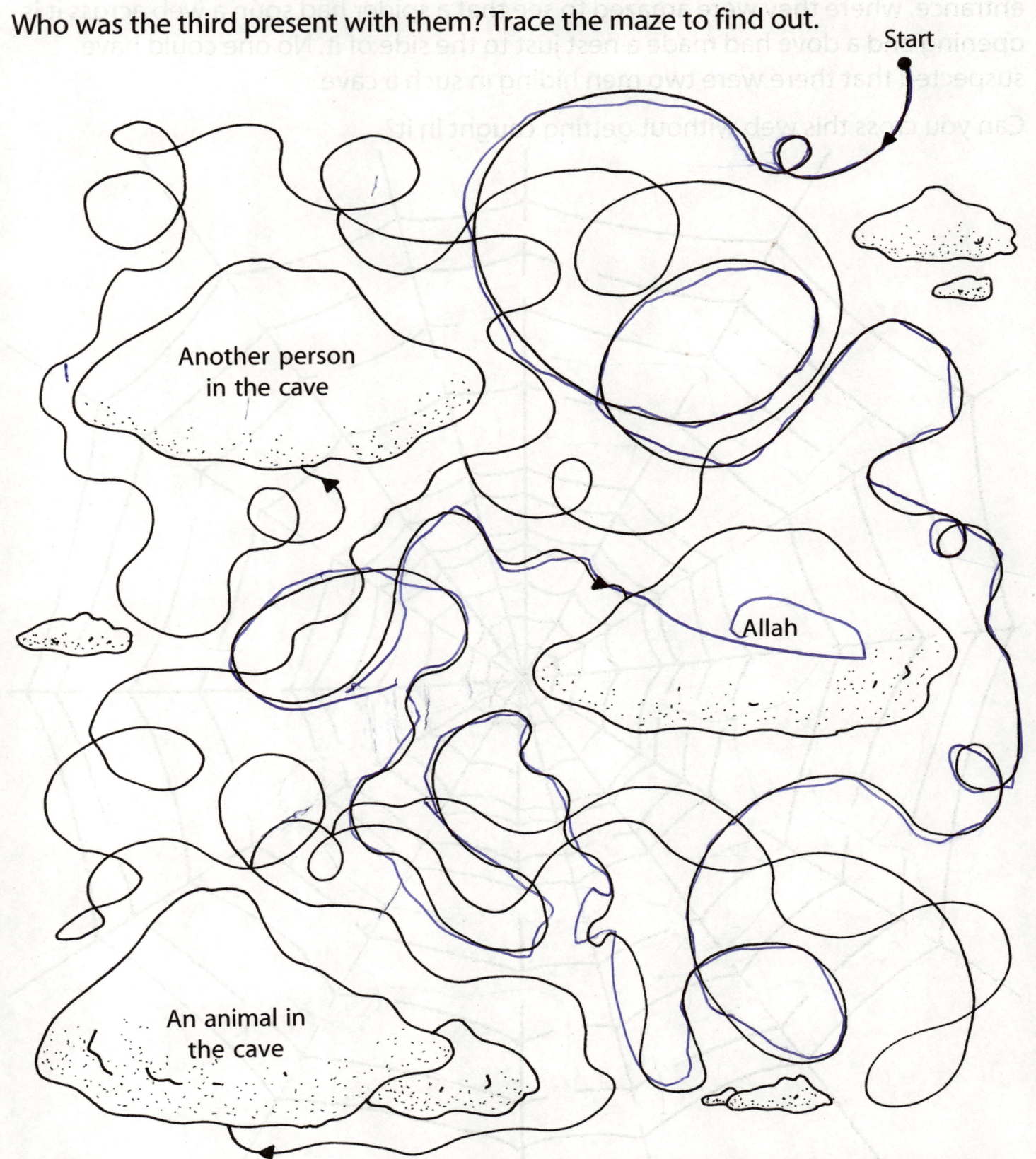

Start

Another person in the cave

Allah

An animal in the cave

The Prophet Muhammad ﷺ replied, "Allah is with us. He will surely protect us."

15 *Sirah Story Mazes: The Prophet Muhammad ﷺ Migrates to Madinah*

© Goodword Books

The search party that had come uptill the entrance of the cave left without looking inside. After sometime, the Prophet and Abu Bakr looked out from the entrance, where they were amazed to see that a spider had spun a web across it is opening and a dove had made a nest just to the side of it. No one could have suspected that there were two men hiding in such a cave.

Can you cross this web without getting caught in it?

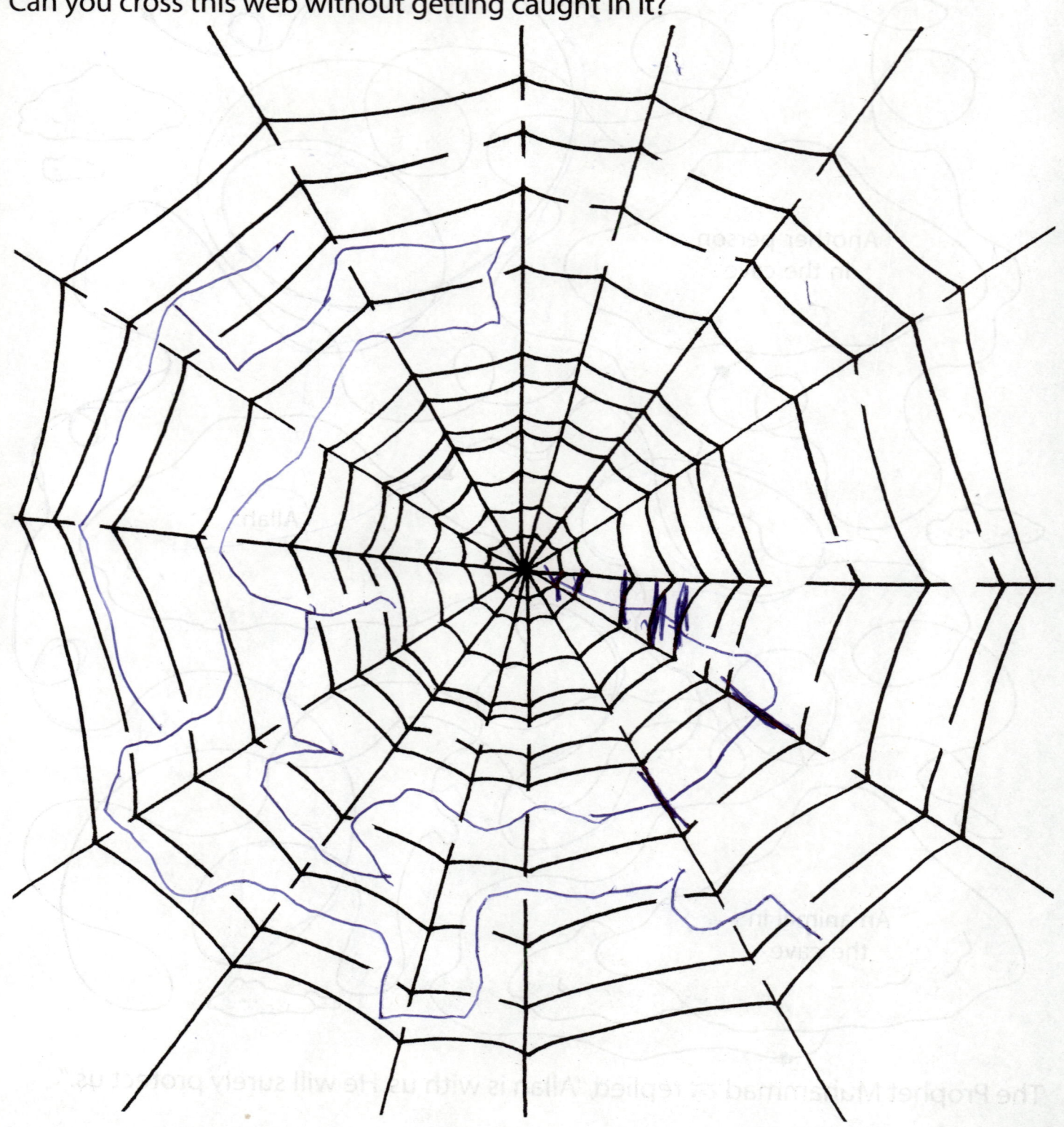

The Prophet Muhammad ﷺ and Abu Bakr continued on their journey. They travelled by night and took a long, winding route to Madinah.

Can you find out which one of these long, winding routes leads to Madinah?

Start

Finish

© Goodword Books

17 Sirah Story Mazes: The Prophet Muhammad ﷺ Migrates to Madinah

It was now 622 A.D., twelve years after the revelation of the Quran. As the Prophet and Abu Bakr rode into the town of Yathrib (now known as Madinah), the people climbed on roof-tops and palm trees to welcome them joyously.

Go from roof-top A to roof-top B.

From that day on, the town of Yathrib known by it's new name.
Trace the maze and write down the letters to find out the new name.

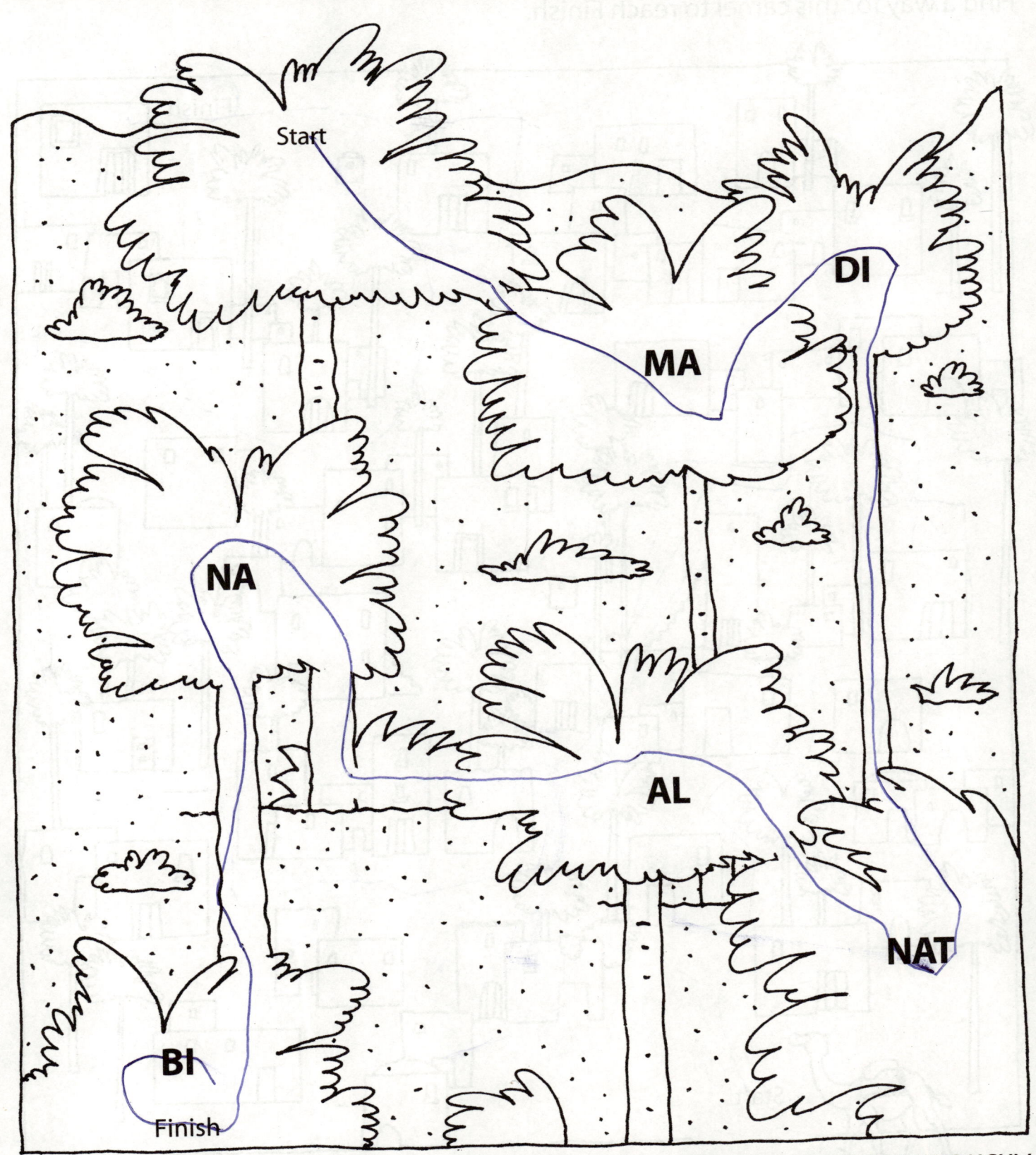

Start

DI

MA

NA

AL

NAT

BI
Finish

Answer: Madinat al-Nabi (which means the City of the Prophet) or Madinah in short.

19 Sirah Story Mazes: The Prophet Muhammad Migrates to Madinah

© Goodword Books

When the Prophet entered Madinah, every citizen wanted him to be his guest. "I shall stay in the house before which my camel stops."

Find a way for this camel to reach Finish.

What is the migration of the Prophet Muhammad ﷺ from Makkah to Madinah famously known as?

Trace the maze and write down the letters to find out.

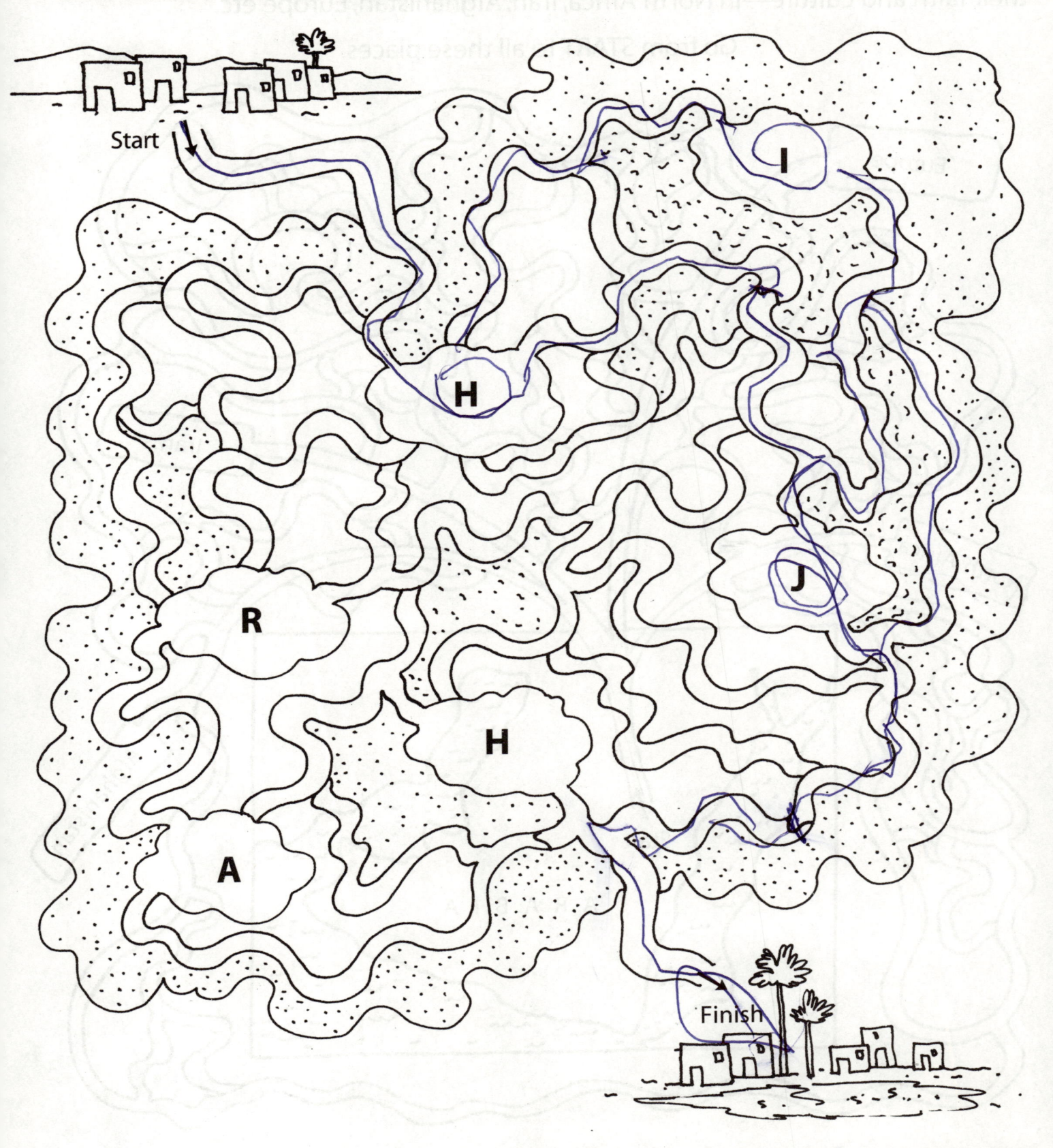

21 Sirah Story Mazes: The Prophet Muhammad ﷺ Migrates to Madinah

© Goodword Books

Hijrah—which means migration—is never for gain, but for the higher purpose of serving Allah. In fact, some yeas later, the Prophet's companions migrated to many places and it was under their influence that whole nations and societies changed their faith and culture—in North Africa, Iran, Afghanistan, Europe etc.

Go from START to all these places.

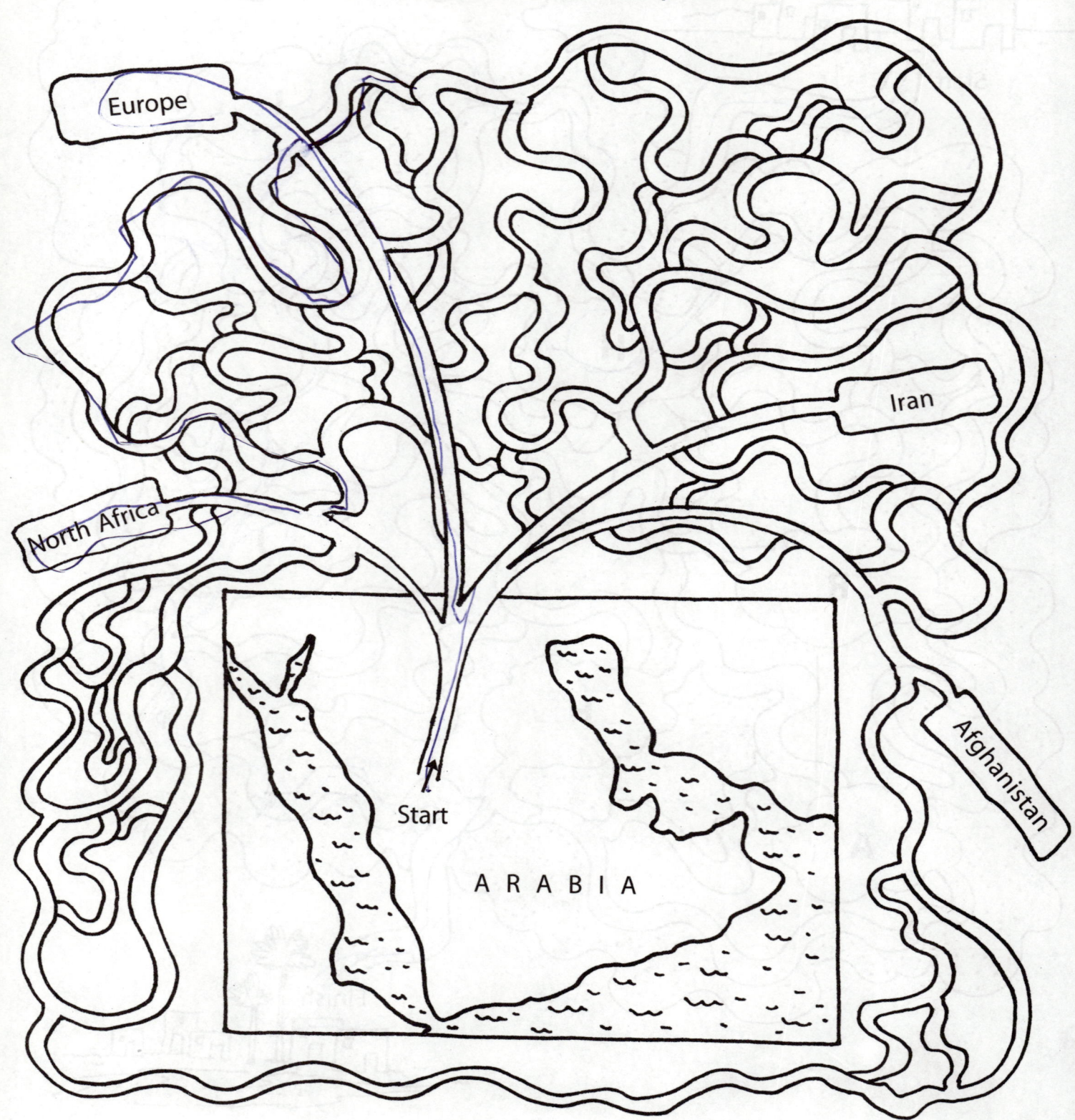

The Prophet's journey from Makkah to Madinah—the Hijrah or migration—was the first real step in the world-wide spread of Islam. That is why Muslims begin their calendar from the year of the Hijrah, 622 A.D.

Reach the finish by following 622.

Year 1 of Hijrah   **622 A.D.**

Start 622	622	570	622	622	622	621	628	570	595
632	622	622	622	621	622	595	610	632	605
610	622	605	632	610	622	622	622	622	621
605	622	622	570	605	628	610	632	622	628
621	605	628	595	622	622	622	622	622	632
621	622	622	622	622	621	610	632	622	628
622	622	605	621	610	628	570	610	622	622
622	628	570	622	622	622	595	632	595	622
622	622	622	622	610	622	628	622	622	622
622	610	632	595	605	622	595	610	632	595
622	622	622	622	610	622	622	622	622	Finish 622

Do you know why the other dates given in this maze — 570, 595, 605, 610, 621, 628 and 632 A.D. — are also of great importance in the history of Islam? If not, look up in a book or ask your parent or teacher.

© Goodword Books   Sirah Story Mazes: The Prophet Muhammad Migrates to Madinah

Due to the presence of the Prophet Muhammad ﷺ, Madinah had become a great Islamic Centre. Here the Prophet built the first mosque, a meeting place of the faithful, now known as Masjid an-Nabawi or the Mosque of the Prophet.

Start

Finish

© Goodword Books

24 Sirah Story Mazes: The Prophet Muhammad ﷺ Migrates to Madinah

The Prophet's departure to Madinah made the Quraysh ever angrier. Two years after the Prophet's migration a large army of the Quraysh approached Madinah to attack the Muslims. They camped at a group of well near Madinah. Here the Prophet fought them with a small group of believers and against heavy odds defeated them.

Be wary of the weapons as you try to reach the FINISH.

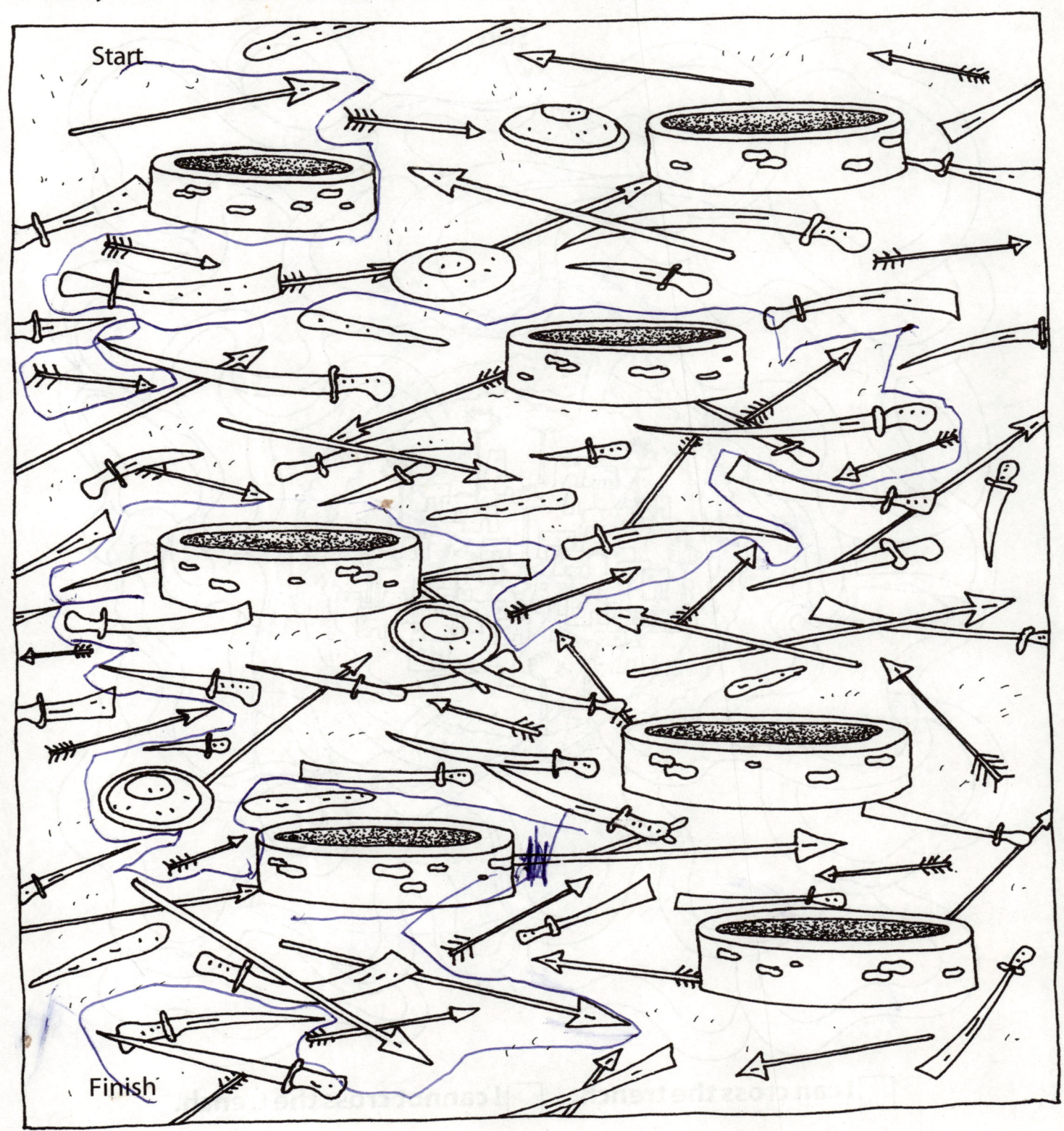

Their defeat further enraged the Quraysh and they came to attack more times. In one of the battles the Prophet was advised by a wise Persian companion to dig a trench around Madinah. 3000 men dug for 20 days to build the trench. When a huge Makkan army arrived they could not cross the trench.

See if you can cross the trench into the town and then tick (✓) the right answer.

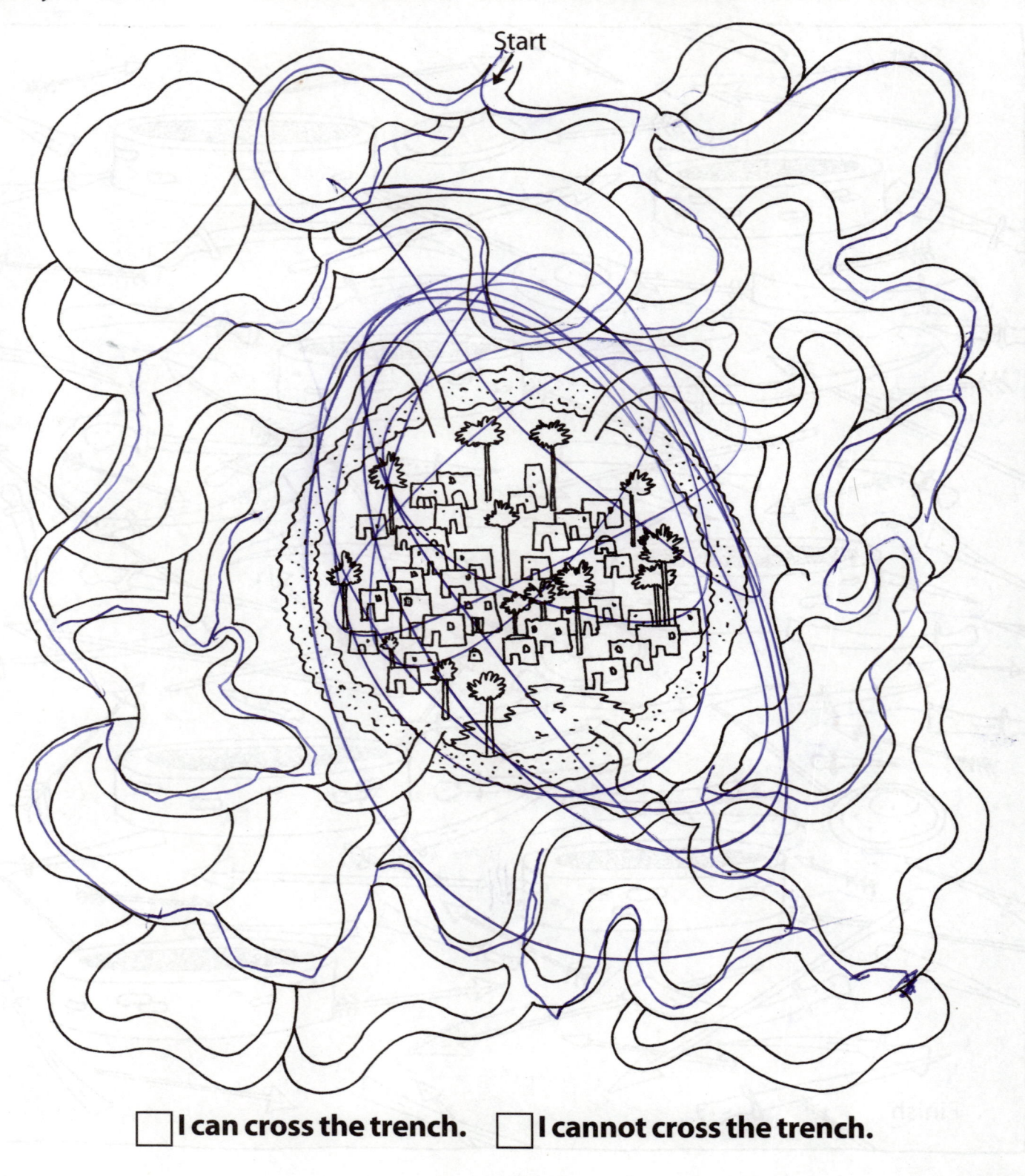

☐ I can cross the trench.   ☐ I cannot cross the trench.

The Makkans camped for a whole month outside Madinah but still could not succeed. Then suddenly a furious wind blew all their tents and stores away. They decided to retreat.

Try not to get blown away in the wind as you try to reach FINISH.

In the 6th year of Hijrah (628 A.D.), the Prophet signed a peace treaty with the Makkans, called the Treaty of Hudaybiyyah. The Muslims were now free to make a pilgrimage to Makkah and stay for three days.

It was a clear victory of the Prophet.

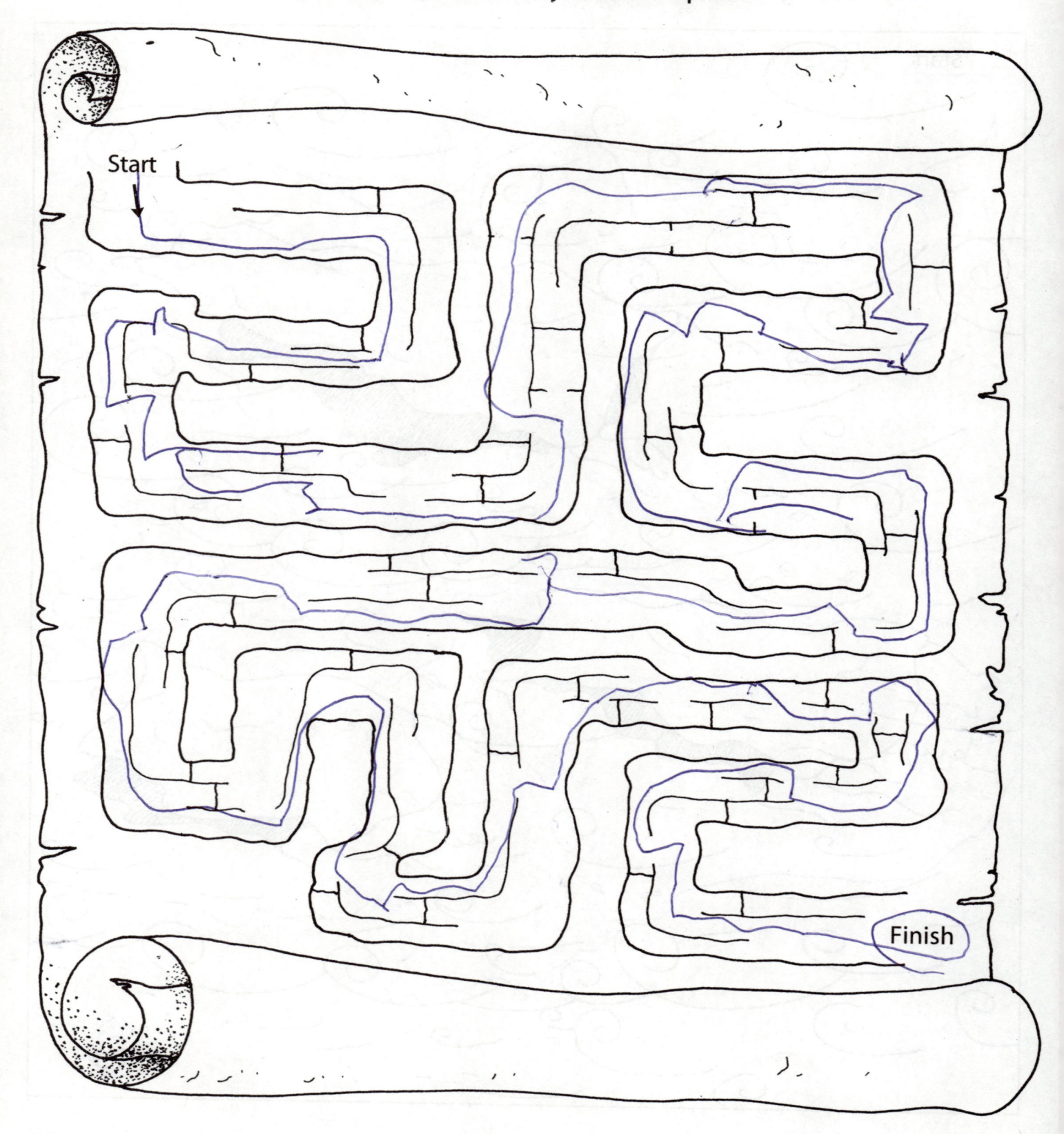

Zakat, or almsgiving is one of the pillars of Islam. The Prophet preached that everything, including our wealth belongs _____.
Trace the maze to find out.

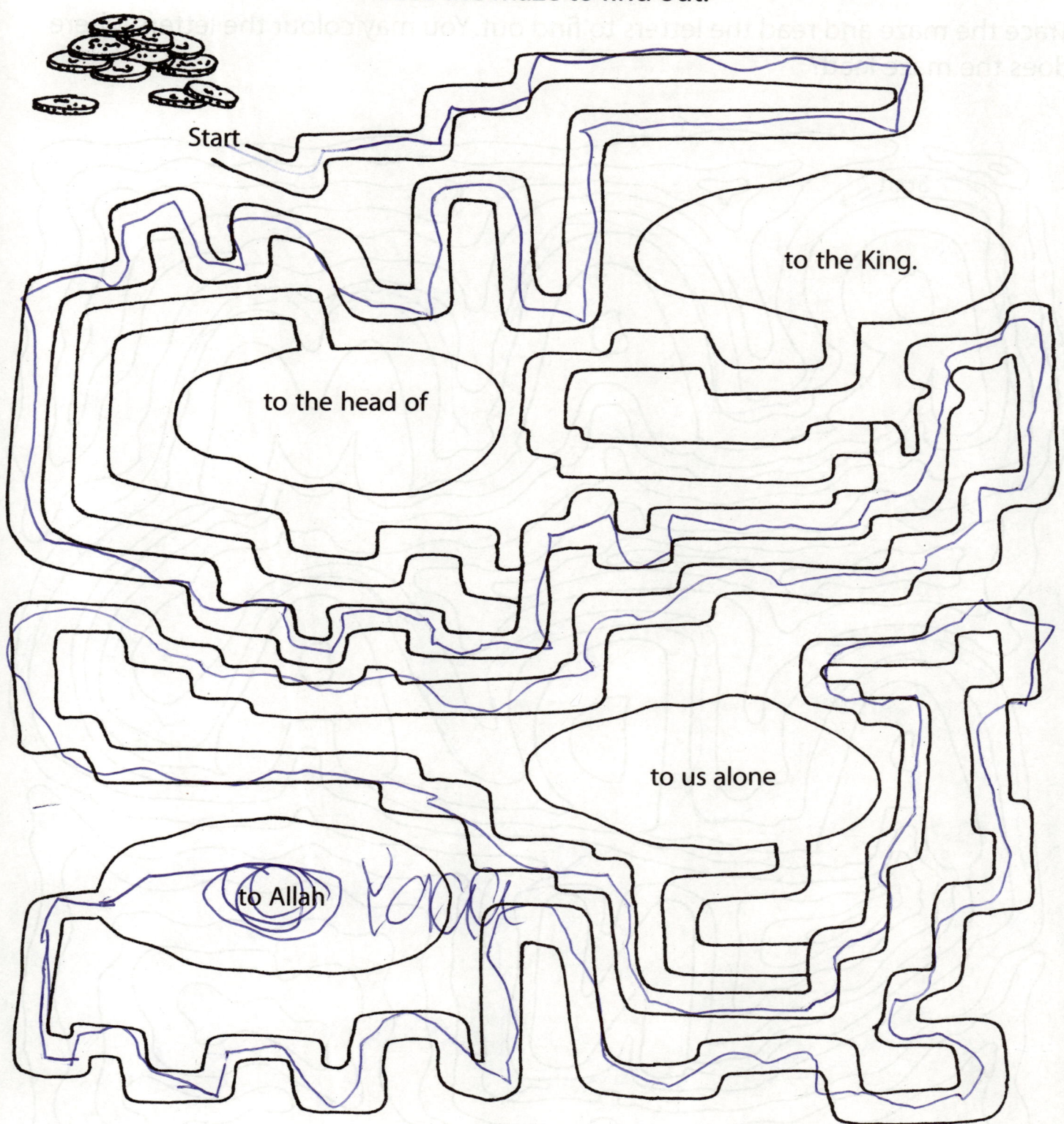

to the King.

to the head of

to us alone

to Allah

The Prophet taught that we must regularly give a portion of our wealth to the poor and the needy.

© Goodword Books   29   Sirah Story Mazes: The Prophet Muhammad ﷺ Migrates to Madinah

Another pillar of Islam is Sawm or fasting. To teach his followers self-discipline, and to recall the month in which the first Quranic verses were revealed, the Prophet organized regular fasting during the month of _____.

Trace the maze and read the letters to find out. You may colour the letters where does the maze lead?

The Muslims who came from Makkah to Madinah were empty-handed while the Muslims of Madinah had houses, lands, orchards etc. But the Madinan Muslims shared everything they had. Such self-sacrifice is called Israr. The Quran says that those who possess this quality will prosper.

Here is a Madinan house with doors open in welcome.

Start

Finish

© Goodword Books   31   Sirah Story Mazes: The Prophet Muhammad Migrates to Madinah

Once a man came to the Prophet ﷺ and said, "O Prophet, by God, it is my earnest desire to go to heaven. Tell me what should I do for this to happen." What did the Prophet reply.

Solve the maze and read the answer below.

"SPEAK THE TRUTH"

The Prophet ﷺ replied, "Speak the truth." For only when a man speaks the truth he does good deeds. And only then he can be sure of entrance to Paradise.